root of light

root of light

poems by
michelle doege

SHANTI ARTS PUBLISHING

BRUNSWICK, MAINE

Root of Light

Published by Shanti Arts Publishing

Designed by Shanti Arts Designs

Artwork is by Penny Poole and used with her permission.

Deena Metzger, "Return" from *Ruin and Beauty: New and Selected Poems*. Copyright © 2009 by Deena Metzger. Reprinted with the permission of The Permissions Company, LLC on behalf of Red Hen Press, redhen.org. Permission also granted by author.

"Air"—after Laurie D. Graham's *Rove* (Hagios Press, 2013).

"Tree Body, Meditations"—after Phyllis Webb's *Naked Poems* (Periwinkle Press, 1965).

"Home"—italicized words from John Lent's poem "Home," *Cantilevered Songs* (Thistledown Press, 2009); used with his permission

Shanti Arts LLC
193 Hillside Road
Brunswick, Maine 04011
shantiarts.com

Printed in the United States of America

ISBN: 978-1-956056-47-1 (softcover)

Library of Congress Control Number: 2022943466

for my father,

Joseph Vernon Doege

When you go
to the dark place,
you must come back
singing,
the note inscribed
on your palm,
song written
on your hand,
the way trees
grow about the
shape of wind.

—*Deena Metzger*

Contents

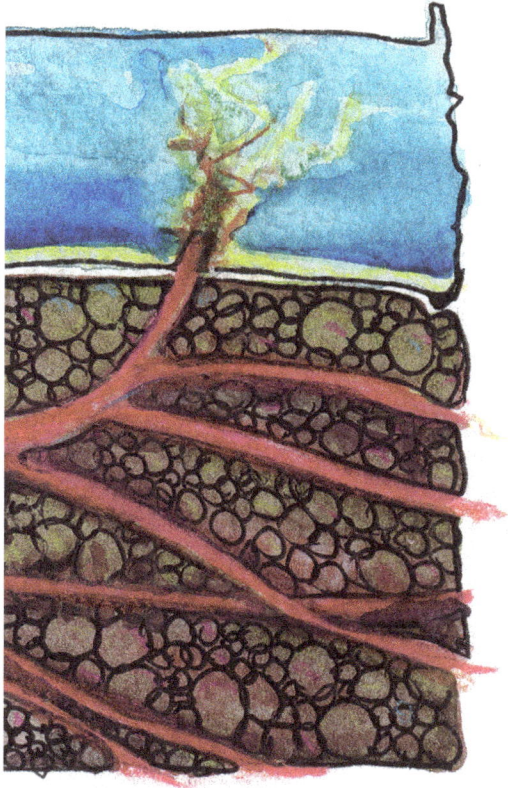

greening

Flame & Ember

for Vindu

cross the borders of bodies:
                    mine—a cave you crawl into
                                        hibernate for your winter.
                            yours—a cocoon wrapped
                    around my metamorphosis.
my love, take me to your taj, your paradise
                    your brown swollen breast at my temple
            and I will walk you into my wilderness
                            of trees quaking each other into a storm.
our family branch of curries and pot pies
                    ragas and sagas and the heart of a working class
        yogi-cowboy-girl dancing with a bard-of-a-witch.
nigeria minnesota india new mexico ottawa london vernon
                    the moving truck stops here:
                                        in our peapod of a home
                        siva watching over us
        dancing over our heads & swirling us into flames
                                the cliff outside our window
                    steep as when we first jumped off.

Awaken, India

Impressionist haze   in distant sky,
      sand colored light
                on adobe wall
The skin loosens   on bone,
      muscles of the body
             release like rain.

Something in the chaos of the air:

Machine gun horns on city streets,
vendors shouting pakoras, papers,
coconut milk—the aroma of deep
fried batter, of urine—   rattles

the body
                unfurling
        in this soft slant
           of light.

Off Shoots

Branches of a banyan shoot out over the Atlantic
    drop thin roots into unfamiliar soil.

        Arabic chants hover Manhattan as men face Mecca
            press their foreheads into the cool mosque floor.

    Polish is spoken on entire streets in Toronto—red leather
      boots bought with hands flailing in the air.

        Dusted in chapatti flour, grinding masala on marble
          cumin, turmeric—one line of the family seed.

The veins of her grandmother's hands, hers—as she
    strokes blue crescent moon onto canvas white.

Must You Cross a Border

Pack a bag—put in a statue of Buddha or a beaded
leather pouch, your grandmother's wedding ring
or an ancestor's earthenware pot. Must you embody
a blizzard to reach your new land? Must you be torn
apart before you can be put back together again?

Few Roots

Three stories above my head
my wife watches laugh-out-loud
comedy airing out of Montreal.
I can almost   hear her
laugh   out   loud
in this silence, between
intermittent squawks
of ducks and geese.

We are at a spa resort
in the south Okanagan
to celebrate Christmas
[whatever that means to
a lesbian-Indian-pagan-
couple with no kids
& few roots securing us
to some place on this earth,
anymore.]   Determined
                to do what is still
    or what sets us on fire.

We microwave Amy's frozen lasagna
      on Christmas eve   [no rules
        no deliriously   desirous
           cooks   in the house.]
      Noodles speared
              from a card-board box
        as we grin at each other
            over Italian Prosecco.

Now,
                          in this hot tub
        for one
this snow-globe   of a world
        luminous sky
                       in my throat.
     Flakes melt   on my upturned
        face
            to the window—
        my love,
           home.

Ghost Ranch

High on this table-top mesa
of copper-colored rock,
shallow veins of a pinon
beneath orange-dusted feet.
Limbs barren and twisted
wrestled by desert winds,
old arthritic fingers
reaching for the sun.

Those who say the desert
is dead, nothing can grow
here   have not stood
sun burned   & baked
       alive to the way
           of rocks.
Have not stood
       wind blown & wild
a tumbleweed
                     raging
    across a desert floor.

That Boy

You lie in bed at night
& want to dream of the boys,
so want to dream of the boys.
And yet, only girls dance in
the sandy beach of your mind,
slide into your body like fish
swimming in the clear light
of water. Like the tingling
moist music riding high
on your thighs. You watch
the boy in the van drive
away with his girl. Imagine
them later sprawled out on
the mattress after three beers
and two shots of Mad Dog.
Finger-tips wander on soft
skin, on supple curve of hip.
Hearts stomp as their breath
gallops across an open field
of yellow. And later still,
dreaming into the naked body
of the other—they will sleep;
they will wake. You want
to be that boy. You so
want to be that boy.

Twirl

Two girls climb the rungs nailed to an old oak tree
wiggle their way through the fort door—pretend

to pull the curtains, to hang a do not disturb sign
as they lower twin bodies onto a velour blanket.

Bare limbs entwine like the trunk of a banyan—
curious & quivering lips mingle   tongues

twirl as they tell themselves they prepare
for the boys   the oak tree leaves
                                        quake.

Wildwood

wild   wide & open

               like the sky   wild.

         like crevice   in that valley   wide.

               like wide-eyed child

holding leaf   or stone

               or tiny purple flower

          wild.   ain't no stoppin'

              that tree—   wild

that cat—   yes,

              that cat is *wild*.

run wild.   run & leap

              off that cliff

                       wild

       into that lake—

                 tear off your clothes

        wild

             as you leap.

Tree Sap

Thick sap
seeps
through her veins
like a snail
on a limb.
Legs—
stiff roots
& tiny tentacles
deepening
into the earth.
Buds burst
inside   her chest.
Her birdsong
throat   rattles
as tree sap
drips
between
her legs.

Oak Tree

Oh oak tree out my living room window
at the age of thirteen. Your trunk, strong & solid
as the generations hovering our family home.
I stand under you—spine against your trunk,
look up to see your limbs sway in ethereal blue.
I pick up an acorn, put it deep in my pocket—
keep it there for the next seventeen years.

Tonewood

The tonewood of this guitar is in the bone of her body.
Her body   in the sound of this sanding.

A dark shadow of song rises from inside her chest
as arms push sandpaper   deeper into wood:

Go with the grain, back & forth, back & forth, again & again.
The Catalpa is a fine tonewood—a tree misnamed, renamed

from kutuhlpa to catawba to catalpa by the Cherokee, the Iswa
by a confused Botanist named Scopoli. A phoenix of a tree

with heart-shaped ears for leaves. Leaves when devoured
by worms return again & again from sawdust & from ash.

Her family's house of skeletons sits on the hill. Her father's 45s
melt in the attic. Her mother's song, swallowed by the oven.

She rubs circles around the guitar's mouth, rubs harder—
that fiery bird hidden inside that gaping hole.

The music reverberates—   rattles her body
as the Catalpa leaves rustle overhead,

Listen:

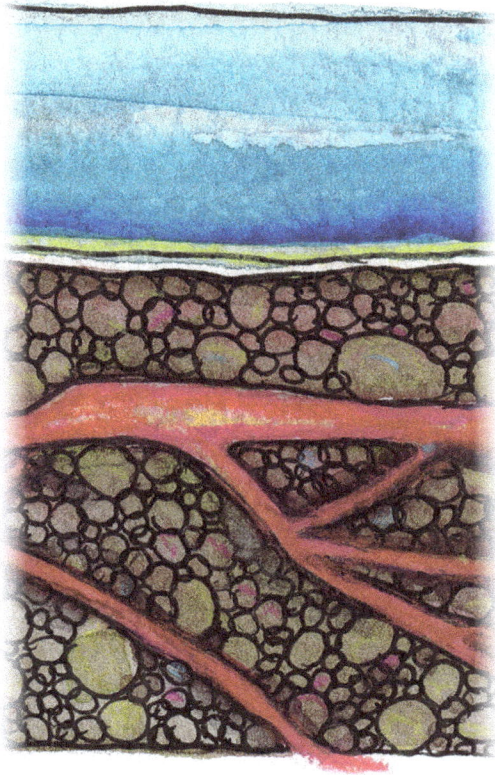

severed limbs

Air

Say pine beetle. Say eating away a tree from the inside
out. Say dead branches the color of red. Say raging
forest fire swallows the side of a mountain, igniting
a house like a marshmallow. Say orange green haze
and red sun. Red moon. Say that for sixteen days.

Canoe across Sugar Lake like paddling on a film set
for a Canadian afterlife. Say you can't see the mountain.
Can't see your tent. Can't find your way home. Smoke
blowing up from Washington. Trees like toothpicks.

Say fires don't need passports to cross borders. Say
fire insurance. Say you can never replace your home.
Say you can only see mountains and hazy rolling ridges
as you drive the BC highways. Now say you can only see
clear-cuts. Can't take your eyes off the gaping wounds.

Say Coquihalla. Say Pacific Free Trade Agreement.
Say—yeah! We can now ship more trees to China.

Say beauty that splits your heart in two. Say waterfall.
Say pine forest wall of green. Say plant trees across
the wreckage. Say pop them into the ground as fast
as you can. Say try to find earth between rock & stump.

Say soil. Say barren. Say landslide. Say grow. Say
red-orange leaves on forest floor. Say Thanksgiving.
Say harvest. Say pine tree mirage on silent lake.
Say emerald.   Say breathing.   Say air.

Clear Cut

Hazy layers unfold in the horizon as our plane
jet-sets over the Monashees.   Our bodies,
weightless and dreamy as the white mist
hovering each jagged edge and blue.

Your palm, warm on my thigh as my forehead
presses into the oblong window pane. I peer
onto the top of a mountain face—notice veins,
interlocking arteries, a landscape divided

by logging roads. To lay a leafless tree flat
single dimensional upon your skin—limbs
and branches roadways   arteries
taking away [not bringing] new life.

Leaves a patchwork quilt, varying shades
of green upon your skin. Leaves fresh
wounds—some lichen and grown over,
some the color of the dry, cracked earth.

[A Prayer]

Follow the stream to the edge of the property
& set up your tent there   [there
far away from the other tents huddled
into a circle at this four-day yoga retreat.]
Carry camp gear from your car.   Walk
towards the circle of trees [not the circle
of yogis].   Seek shade in this BC
mountain meadow.   Poke short pole
into short pole—   thread blue dome
of a home.   Face chairs towards
a stream you cannot see. Sit & listen
to the chant of water on rock.   Store
food in your trunk. Go to bed early.
Spoon   your wife.

Your wife who pops in earplugs
so does not hear the sound of water
on rock, the crack of twigs underfoot.
She does not wake to a screech,
a whirl, a buzz   & a shriek
so you nudge your wife in her ribs.
Bodies respond   [all at once]
to nails on blackboard   drill
on teeth   a siren screaming
down the street   as chainsaw
rips   into wood.

[I am in the forest   & I hear.]

Up by five   [saws still whirling].
Meditation by six [trees still crashing].
One hour for coffee and to use
the composting toilet [fingernails,
                      drill   & siren]
while sitting   on the pot.

Stroll into meditation space,
lay down blanket, place zafu
at the center. Face the front
of the room [smile at your
teacher].   Sit on zafu,
legs crossed   hands
on thighs   [in mudra]
hold the sky.   Focus
        on your body,
let the world fall away.
[a whirl & a shriek]
Hold
        that pose.

Body of Fire

for Uncle Patrick

I imagine those peach bell-bottoms
making quite a wave on a Saturday night
at the Gay 90s, swooning your chicken
legs to Marvin Gaye's *Let's Get it On*
during happy hour, hoping to hop
out to dinner with some fine chap.
Dreaming of later, and later still
as you dance.   Your pant legs
still grooving in the family photo
at your parents' Wisconsin farm
better aligned with those apple trees
than your Catholic farm stock
heading out to the fields
to harvest soy or wheat.

You try to join the church,
all those priests & altar boys
tugging at your trembling faith.
On one dark night you stand
ejected into an alleyway
before God and all things holy
told to go marry,   go find
a good wife.   Instead,
you enlist in the Army
the impossibility of all
those muscular thighs.

We peer out the living room
window   watch your bell-
bottoms spill out the rental car
door. My brothers warned
not to be with you alone.
                    To never
be with you   alone.

On those tangled nights
when I dream of the girls
I think of you—my body
of fire   whispers:

> *drinks too much,*

>   *drugs*

>   *gay*   *stay away.*

You, cut from the tree

                              severed

          dead at forty-two

                    stumbling into

          some Michigan street

                              too many drinks

                    or snorting up a line.

     Ran over & killed

                              by the blood

          of your own

                    pulsing desire.

As Straight

Grey tree-trunks stripped of bark
lay scattered like pick-up sticks
strewn onto the living room carpet
on a Saturday night. The dad
pops popcorn, melts butter
plops the bowl into the middle
of his circle of kids, red-onesie
pajamas, a superman symbol
on his boy's chest.

                The girl
will grow, sit next to her father
in his Ford 150, head to Knox
to pick up lumber to expand
their shrinking family-home.
She will climb ladders onto
rooftops, nail shingles. She
will learn to pull back her leg
as she revs-up the circular saw.
He taught her:

              To hold a 2x4
at an angle, eye the edge down
to the floor, make sure the board
is as straight as a small-town boy.
This quiet cowboy of a man
can imagine nothing more—
only a girl swooning over
a boy whose blood gyrates
with Loverboy and beer.

Fall

Never fall.
Never fall
                    in love
        [with a woman].
Never fall
                    [in the land
    of the free]
                for another woman
        [especially]   a woman
            from India.

Black Ink

Families with brown skin line up at the border office:
                              A child folds-over
a shoulder, a mother & father whisper quiet words
wait—   fingers pressed into black ink,
record of the family body.   The contents
of their car—suitcases cracked open like lives,
ties and pressed shirts spill over.   A car seat
taken apart like a Lego set.   Rimless tires
lie tired on the ground. My Indian [now] wife
reaches her golden hand towards the guard
                              finger pressed into black ink.
His finger now pointing at my chest:
                                        Who is she?
We stand shoulder-to-shoulder—   mute.

Mallet on Wood

Draw a border. Enforce a line. Put up a fence.
Call the reporter. Face immigration at the border.
Yes, our relationship is real—here: our apartment
lease, records of phone calls to India, utility bills,
civil union papers. Friends' letters: we have known
them together, forever. Here—a sworn testament
of our love. Your honor, pound mallet on wood
use your power   keep us [to-gether].

O Canada

white.   white out.   can't see
        in front   of   truck.
              around   the next
      no apartment   neighborhood
           not   one friend.
no brother   sister.
       no job.   we have   no jobs.
          we see a country.   a country
     said   yes.
a country   welcomed
        fought   pounded
     a large   wooden desk.
now,
          a red
                leaf.

Power Lines

A fence runs up and down the property line. Mine,
yours. You mow, I rake. The divide clear. Your tree
wanders wildly into my airspace, threatens to yank
the gutters off the side of my house. I have a right to cut
your branches in my air. A Ukrainian couple in Canada
heads to the nursery to buy a baby Oak, to plant into
this new land of home. They bow their heads, offer
blessings in their sharp-edged words: *may these roots
go deep, always connect us to our war-torn Ukraine.*
Forty years on and the court date lingers. They refuse
to cut the bark that has wrapped around their bodies
as tree branches yank at the power lines
like the movable borders of home.

Tree Trimmer, A Quote

A body is not meant to be cut in half.
He runs his pointed finger up and down
the median line of his body like a circular saw.

He pushes his right arm into the air like a limb.
If you cut it off right here—hand clenched
in a fist—it will not sprout again at the stub.

All that energy's gotta go somewhere.
Where's all that energy gonna go?

Branches will shoot out sprouts, grow
four to five feet each year. Truth is:
trees aren't meant to be trimmed.

My tree. Your tree. Your neighbor's tree.
Your trunk. Limbs that cross my fence.
Gotta stop thinking like that. Gotta do

what's right for the tree. In the end,
you do what you want. In the end,
I'll do what you tell me to do.

He clenches his forearm with his hand.
If you cut the limb off right here, right
here—showing me where he will cut:

All that energy's gotta go somewhere.
Where's all that energy going to go?

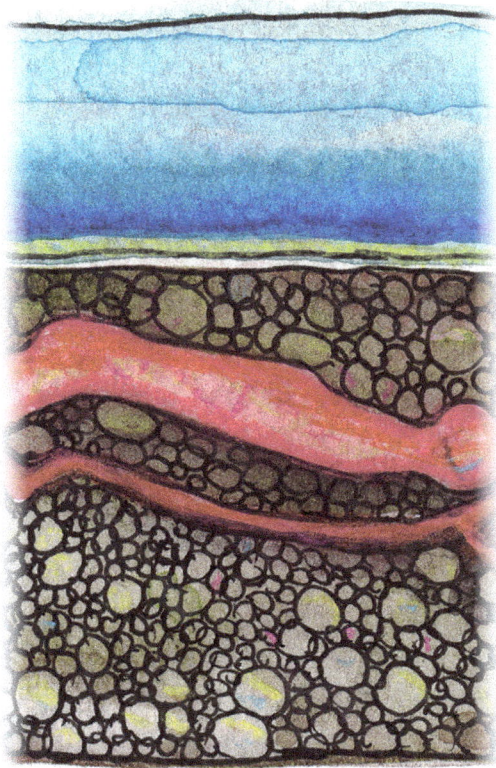

oak tree, always

Two Years

Packs of deer, entire families, feed on the grass
in the graveyard—meander between headstones
and my body, as if my body were already a stone.

> Deer wander the ravine, the grassy slopes
> near my home—heads bow to the ground
> on my walk to the top of Turtle Mountain rock.

> One head lifts, gazes at me mid-stride. I stand
> startled—see my dad's eyes in the eyes of this deer
> his soft glow emanating from muscle and bone.

Deep in the wild of my dream, a gunshot blasts a deer.
I run frantic through a forest, lay my dad's bleeding head
on my thigh—gaze down into his pleading eyes.

> A sturdy buck towers at the top of Turtle Mountain
> rock—ambles to the edge, stares down on me
> as I sip morning coffee in my living room chair.

> I am beginning to believe like the Celts—that you
> have come back to me, an intermediary between
> worlds. I walk to the window and meet you there.

A deer's bulk of a body lays broken, mangled
on the side of the road. He struggles to lift his
smashed skull, stares into my oncoming car.

Circular Saw

for Poppo

I cannot look at your wooden lamp
                              I cannot hold this hammer in hand
   perched at the end of my couch
                        swing it back behind my ear
     & not see your large hands
                     & not feel your blood in my blood
      gripping fine sandpaper
                  impact of nail into wood
    caressing the wavy grain
                to create my pine bookshelf.

        Circular saw whirling
                blade spinning
        [yours & mine]
     the smell of burnt wood
          cigarette smoke and sweat
    sawdust on our tattered shoes.

I cannot look at the wooden chest
    [made by you]
                cannot be in my writing studio
                 [built by me]
    & not see your sturdy arm
         perfect pine floors & spruce ceiling beams
  hammer in hand & nail set to wood
             teak ceiling fan & old wooden desk
     & not feel the solid oak presence of you.

Strut

I wait for the man but the man does not come
so I wield the hammer in my own hand. I strut
into Home Depot sporting my Om t-shirt,
knee poking out of tattered jeans as I stroll
on over to aisle 23. Men in orange aprons
rush to my side—I quickly throw them a line
like rebar or stud finder or 2 x 3 spruce to add
depth for R19 insulation to meet CMHC code.
I order loads of lumber to be delivered to my door,
eye and measure and mark and rev-up the circular
saw—drill and wire, hang and hammer, hover
on a ladder to tack high ceiling beams. I construct
forms, wire rebar, mix cement into a five-gallon
pail to pour like my wife's birthday cake
into a pan. Three builders stop by [did you
imagine them men?] to give their best
building ideas. I sketch-up a diagram
of my own—   paint the walls
adobe, tack pine floor boards, hang
a teak ceiling-fan—push my writing
desk to the window, overlooking
the untamed garden out back.

Click:

Every sock and last pair of underwear is tightly
folded into a box, boxes neatly packed into
the U-Haul. Dining room table and chairs,
living room couch and furniture dusted off,
packed into the back. Honda Civic hoisted
up & hooked on, ready to haul. Orderly.
Organized. As if packing perfectly will
curb the chaos around the next bend.

We snap pictures to freeze-frame
this life. Click: Card tables the length
of dad's living room, the mismatched
plates & silver. Click: family crowding
mashed potatoes & ham, the store-
bought pie. The lesbian couple about
to move to Canada—dad's arms
encircling their shoulders: Click.
A Minnesota picture book, stained-
glass candle holder   a flame
for the other side
                    of the border.

Border Crossing

Our countries   divide us
    like the stillness   inside our warm cab
      and the snow   pounding
        against the glass.
Hour after hour   hands melded to the wheel
    snow needles want to pierce my face.
   We become delirious
            mesmerized
     hardly aware
          if we are still
      on the road.

    The snow flails at my eyes, my eyes, my eyes
          hypnotized:

Dad swings his hammer to build our family home.

    Me at three under our weeping willow tree.

My university degrees framed up on the wall.

Our immigration lawyer – mouth opening and closing like a puppet:
   "you can't get married; she has no right to immigrate."

    Friends Amy and John and dog Winnie fly by.

Walking slow circles around Como Lake—holding hands
     under our tree, the moon   mid-night.

               Red rock canyons & Georgia O'Keeffe's sky.

          Naked bodies in New Mexico hot springs.

     Great-grandfather sawing trees from his homestead land.

Frothy beer with sister Rosie in an old-world pub.

               Bi-weekly paychecks and U.S. bank accounts.

     Canadian immigration application — bold letters read:
          "Humanitarian and Compassionate Grounds."

               The Mississippi River winding around our truck.

Our lawyer: "Of course she could immigrate if she was a man!"

My mother laughing – flying about in the wind.

Bloodline

High on this mesa
a thousand miles
from home
I gaze
into the sage
valley—
a freeway
like an artery
runs through
my dad's withered arm
[at this very moment]
a thousand miles
receives
the needle,
the chemo—
small cars
racing
in his
veins.

Only

The family doctor orders a series
of tests   hold your breath
Russian roulette.
                    One moment
fingers curl a pencil   tap
                on a keyboard
blood pulsing protruding veins
and then   not.
Bike out of the garage   helmet
secure   rear view mirror fixed
on approaching traffic
then gone.   If lucky,
we travel from root through trunk
sway into the branches
of old age. Fall gracefully,
                    leaf from tree.
No guarantee, this soft exhale:
Live each day.
                    Carpe diem.
Only these fingers,
                            this air.

Doulas

A woman in Ghana [at this very moment] squats and moans, hovers the red earth covered in dry grass, a quilted blanket for her baby to fall softly into this world. One man in Ohio [in this same moment] groans in hospice. What he knows for sure is he had this one life. His Indian friend tries to tells him otherwise. That he has many. That he can come back as a dog, a king or even a trash collector. He doesn't believe—believes he had just this one. Her doula squats next to her, reaches her hand beneath the hanging of her breasts, massages the foothill of her stomach with oil & herbs. They breathe together—breathe & moan & scream while women encircle the tent, call out to the ancestors in song. This man, his bony body lying like mangled metal beneath a white cotton sheet, squirms & wrestles to stay firmly in this world. His children encircle his body. His son massages the thin blue veins on his hand. Others caress his crumpled legs, massage his bloated feet. His daughter whispers into his ear like a song. The baby, now wrapped in her mother's body for months, is ready to enter this red world. They breathe with his breath, moan with his groan. Soft or shallow, long or deep. They hold his breath— howl into the umbilical cord, howl into the florescent light— as life slips his skin.

Sockeye

Red tongues of sumac flutter
on the banks of the Adam's River
as sockeye scurry against the current
the forcefield of home tugging at their fins.
Now, red flames in this river of their birth.

Tourists spill from buses, form a human
current along the river's edge. The smell
of dead fish lingers, water crashes
against rock. The sockeye return here
to die, become food for their young.

Long lenses poke out from bodies
ready to point & shoot. Click: a male
fights for his mate. Click: a female fans
a crevice in stones to lay her pearl eggs.
Yet, not one lens points to the bloated
bellies—lying belly-up in the sun.

Tree Body, Meditations

exhale

                             inhale

           breathe in

                                          out.

                                                                roots

                                            embryonic

                                                    tentacles.

                                      thin blue veins

                                          suckling

                                                  the earth.

.

             air   to leaf

leaf

                 air

      taproot

               into soil

    black.

trunk energy

cruising

sugar & water

a two way

street.

stand
strong & stoic
in the middle
you trunk, you
holding it all
together.

a leaf

flutters

to grass,

brown.

Absence of Light

Tree shadows walk across the backyard
       toward the house as the sun folds
over the mountain face. The heavy weight
       of winter presses into our skin
even birds clench their beaks. We squirm
       inside this fertile darkness
no light at the end of this tunnel, at least
       that we can see. Too quiet
too alone. Even for a God. Our faces
       aglow in our TV screens.

root of light

Seeds

Draw a line around a cut-block
like a country, a border around
Crown land. Buy and sell and
trade and barter—the highest
bidder takes the order.
The forest echoes:
> *we cannot buy or sell*
> > *we belong to*
> *remember this sap.*

A tree falls in the forest, yes.
But always,
                    seeds.

Blue-god

Fluorescent light fragments like the sun's rays over
our tiny cubicles—luminescent, but not from the sky.
Locked to this keyboard, handcuffs at our wrists
on a thirty-minute break we will walk towards blue.
Instead of picking rocks from our grandfather's field
we plant formulas and data into an Excel spreadsheet
determined to save this world with our round facts.
The smell of hay in the barn, the silhouette of cows
walking up the grassy slope into a blood-orange sky.

       Petals of Georgia O'Keeffe's morning-glory
       blossom over a white wall in Sante Fe.
       She wants us to notice the flower. To see
       this blue-god of a flower,   hanging
       next to the skeletal pelvis of a single cow.

Pacing the living room, baby bouncing on her hip
blue tooth in her ear as she talks to her mom.
Water boiling on the stove for mac and cheese
frozen fried fish in the toaster oven, ready to ding.
She catches a glimpse of the blood-red sun,
the warmth of the barn aglow in this room.
Her baby's face, deep in the crevice of her neck.

Mirror

The dock pokes out over the water
like a long beak. We sit, legs crossed
the water, silent—still. Our faces
reflect back to us the world. We
almost believe there is a God in
this large mirror. So many years
of slicing hoe into dirt, a crevice
for seeds to sprout miraculously
from the tilled earth.

Arteries

Place your palm on this tree
feel her pulse. Cracked skin
on the back of your hand
crevices in bark
                    in wood.
Roots that weave
                    into this world
            round   reach
for the centre
            & then through.

                    All these roots   arteries
                                        and thin veins
                        a tangled web   of a world.
                    Our great-great
                                                grandmothers
                                    honored the tree
                        bowed down   to the tree—
                                        their words
                                    vibrate
                                        our tongues.

Grove, Old World

No Jesus Christ or preacher man,
just these trees in a sacred grove
to walk to alone or with a mother,
a brother. Trees deep in the belly
of a forest—a place to go to
when a baby is born, or
stillborn. A marriage
or a death, the sowing
or the harvest of wheat.
Trees to pause at, to pray:
a remembering not yet asleep.

Generation after generation
until this link is broken
in the new world. In this new
world where we sit on polished
pews—gaze out wooden window
frames, a cedar-cross hovering
from on high in this house
of God.   Spines meld
into wood   tree sap
traverses our bodies—
flows from the tips
of our limbs.

Avebury

Sarsen stones cast shadows
        on small seekers
who warm their backs
        on the towering
rock that swallowed
        the midday sun.

Silbury Hill

Field of ocean green
      mound pregnant with earth
           tall grass whispers
     the ancient chorus
of an eternal breeze.

Assisi

The spirit of St. Francis
echoes off these stone
walls as we sip wine
gaze onto the wooden
church doors—open wide
to release his first Words.

The Rhine

Hildegard of Bingen
wandered these hills
flowing with grapevines
and wine—her body
flooded with green,
with vision & song.

Fields of Wheat

Great-great-grandmother grasps the cross on her rosary
says ten Hail Marys and folds her husband's Sunday suit
into a square, places it next to the linen in the trunk.

Farm fields like empty bowls of wheat, potatoes
strangled—they dream of an ocean to cross.

> *Four generations on and perched at a pub in Rüdesheim*
> *sipping a good hefeweizen and chomping on a schnitzel.*
> *I know I am with my people—the marrow of their bone.*

She will never see again her *mutter* hovering
a steaming pot nor her *vater's* hands grasp a hoe.

The horse-drawn carriage, swallowed in a storm
of dust—they transfer from carriage to train to port
until the ocean opens-up like an afterlife.

Waves roll in, smash against the side of the ship
the lines the lines the lines they stand in for ticket,
for medical check, for the sound of a passport stamp.

Their twin bodies wrap around one trunk
the salty mist, a thin film on ashen cheeks.

> *My hips, rolling like these hills of Bavaria. Your fat*
> *German fingers seem to wrap around this stein. Has*
> *your bone really traveled down this long blood line?*

Emigrants with Germany woven into their skin
line up like beads on a rosary   step onto

the nodding ship. Lips murmur—gray water
splashes against the round hole as they push
their trunk alongside the steerage bunk.

A long braid of rope tethers ship to dock
the old to some ghost of new. Unhitched
the shore disappears into a mist of home.

Bodies sway, rise and fall in the waves
tin plate, fork and spoon rattle at their side.

> *We will cross many borders, gouge a pointed plow*
> *into the earth—plant seeds over & over again. A church*
> *steeple rising out of the centre of each new town.*

Practice answering thirty-one questions: *Helga, tventy-seven,*
voman, married to Otto, housevife. Twenty-five dollars? *Yes.*

The rope is anxious to uncoil, to delve deep waters
in search of new land. Stories of lady liberty: The *göttin*
will rise up out of the *wasser* to greet us with a torch.

Sway up the long, steep steps. Doctors peel back
your eyes, your eyes in search of trachoma: *Pass*.
Trunk. Rosary. Tear off 8376/77 as ship turns back.

Buy train tickets. Try to open like the valleys of Bavaria,
your finger now pointed to the centre of a strange map.

> *You will be buried in Minnesota across from a field*
> *of wheat. Döge [now Doege] etched deep into stone.*
> *My feet planted firmly on the grass of your grave.*

Bend over a deep furrow in an ocean of green, drop
seeds into the dark, loamy soil.   My great-great

you cannot see me, nor my own harvest field. My ashes
will be scattered in another mountainous land.   Only,
my father's hazel eyes   released into your light.

Duende

A woman lost in her ravaged world
sits on a bench under the bursting
stars of a magnolia   mutters
words only she understands.

My wife's grey hair, [now] white
petals flowering above her brow—
she is   [like all of us]
both shadow & the blossom.

I wander the bustling sun-soaked
streets, feel an ache in my heart
like a cracked coconut—all the water
spilled out once macheted in half.

So much of my family now sucked
back into the earth—grandparents,
aunts & uncles, parents teetering
with vertigo at the edge of a large hole.

The question always dragging me
around the next blind bend: what
matters most while here, this life?

Hildegard of Bingen sees through
the trees to the greening power,
the energy in the leaf   in me.

I hold all this beauty,   this sadness—
black wings flapping inside my chest
as I walk into this dream of life.

Home

Granddaughter, plant these seeds
into the field of your ancestors
landed in Minnesota, in Iowa.
Plant these potato, carrot
& beetroot seeds brought
over on the boat long before
your parents breathed life
into your lungs. Take
a scythe to *this* land,
plow *this* soil – the soil
that holds the memories
of the Ojibwe. The voices
in my blood they sing:
my child marry and multiply
and live well with the seasons
& the cycles – make *this* land
your home:

> *How we feel that word home*
> *how we imagine what it refers to*
> *how we use it as a redemptive*
> *chorus   whispering.*

When Seamus Heaney's father died
he said the roof blew off his house
blew off the family home. So exposed
was he in the universe, so next in line.

In the names of the blood that dreamed me:
               Henrietta
               Sinon
               Rose
               Albert
               Delia
               Joseph Vernon

The voices in my blood
                         reverberate:
             music of my body.
     Long separated
                    from this chorus of home.
So exposed now
                 in this Okanagan sky:

And I accept this wide sky
               as the roof of my home.
      Called here by some other beat
                    in my blood
         by blue sky & turquoise
beige rock   & sage brush
      & this wide-open heart
          of a landscape.
I accept this longing   & this rootlessness
         this deep sense of place:
     This wildness is my home.

Viriditas

in memory, Hildegard

Steep slopes   grapevines
            wine—the Rhine divides.
The river crossed weekly
            to visit   your sisters.
                  Green:
      the slopes
                        your sisters.

I collided into you
                        in a poem
            eight-hundred-years
                        after your life.
      Gazed at your mandalas.
                        Green:
            a spinning wheel.

The sun   needs the earth
      the plant   the dew.
            Our entire life   exists
                  in one tree.
      Viriditas: green
            & radiant light.

We will wither
                                  like a plant
              in a root cellar
                          until we speak.
          Create:
                              a blossom   blooming
                              a shoot rooted
                                          in light.
                    Green:
                              root of light
                          our song.

It is said your tongue lies
                    in the golden box
          with the bones
                              of your body –
              I see it leaping.
                          Viriditas:
          your tongue,

              flame.

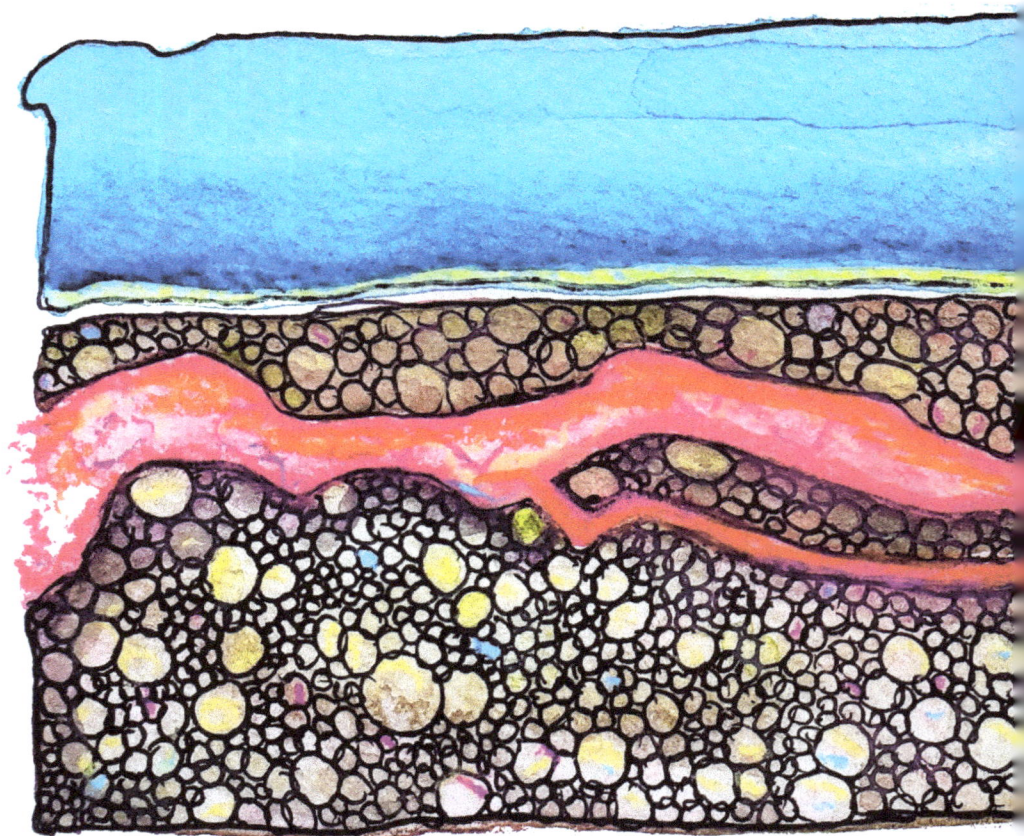

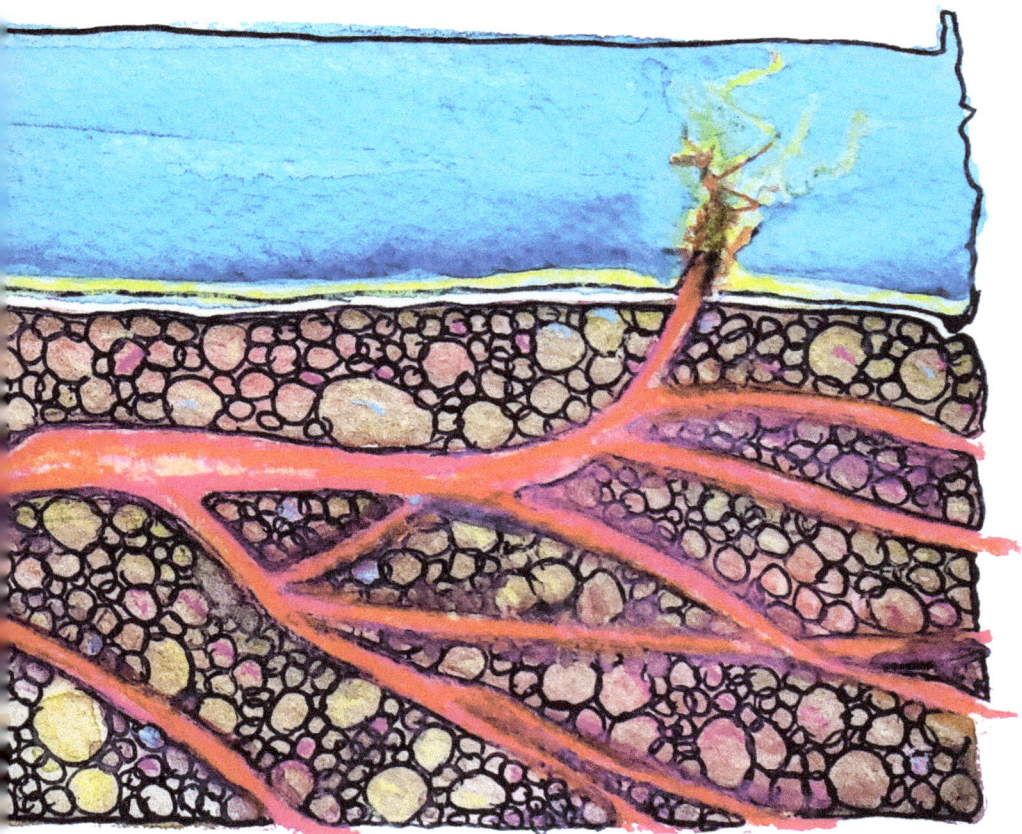

Acknowledgments

My first thanks go out to Heid Erdrich and Cary Waterman, my Augsburg College MFA mentors and earliest encouragers of these poems, helping me to hold the heat and grow, grow into my best poet-self. Thank you to Sharon Thesen for shining your light on this deep vision and poem-song, all along. Special gratitude to Hannah Calder and Chris Thorpe, insightful creative duos who handed me just the right tools to sculpt this larger work of art, on down to the word. To the Spokes of my wheel—Laisha Rosnau, Kerry Gilbert, Natalie Appleton, Kristin Froneman, Karen Meyer, and Hannah— for your inspiration and being a steady breeze at my back.

In great admiration and appreciation for Shanti Arts and publisher Christine Cote, for infusing the world with writing and art that stays true to your mission: nature inspires art / art reveals spirit / spirit changes the world. We need this vision now more than ever. I am honored to be in your circle. My deepest gratitude goes out to Penny Poole—brilliant artist and creative womyn—you bless and honor me each time you draw or paint to my poems.

To my ancestors, my family, who wove the creative into the everyday, often out of necessity—that energy still lives in my bones. To my sister Rosie, thank you for honoring and celebrating my poet-self; your love and support over these many years has meant the world. And to my first and last, always, Vindu Balani—poems are life and sometimes our life becomes a poem—deep gratitude for our journey, for loving me the whole way.

About the Author

MICHELLE DOEGE is a writer of poems and stories, an educator, and a nurturer of any creative community she calls home. She holds an MFA in creative writing in poetry and mixed genre from Augsburg College, Minneapolis, Minnesota. Her poems—both print and video—have appeared in *Why We Write: Poets of Vernon, Smoke & Ash, Possessions: The Eldon House Poems, Avocet: A Journal of Nature Poems, Farm Folk City Folk;* her story "End of a Rainbow" appears in *Wherever I Find Myself: Stories of Canadian Immigrant Women* (Caitlin Press, 2017). Her recent writing has been shortlisted for the *Malahat Review*'s Constance Rooke Creative Nonfiction Award (2021) and earned semi-finalist in the Tulip Tree Publishing Contest (2019). Doege also finds great joy in layering poems with visual art, in broadsides or video collaborations. She currently writes and offers writing workshops in the Okanagan, British Columbia, her home, the green and freshest tendrils of her roots.

To learn more about Doege's writing, creative activities, and workshops, please visit: www.michelledoegepoet.com.

Shanti Arts

Nature · Art · Spirit

·Please visit us online
to browse our entire book catalog,
including poetry collections and fiction,
books on travel, nature, healing, art,
photography, and more.

Also take a look at our highly regarded art
and literary journal, *Still Point Arts Quarterly*,
which may be downloaded for free.

www.shantiarts.com

www.ingramcontent.com/pod-product-compliance
Lightning Source LLC
Chambersburg PA
CBHW042047090426
42733CB00037B/2654